Happy Birthday
To Imogen
Love from
Valerie Bloom
March 30, 2003

ONE RIVER
MANY CREEKS

Poems from all around the world

ONE RIVER
MANY CREEKS

Poems from all around the world

Chosen by
VALERIE BLOOM

MACMILLAN CHILDREN'S BOOKS

For the teachers and children of Frankfield Primary School and
Edwin Allen Comprehensive High School,
and to Penny and Tamara with thanks for their secretarial assistance
- V. B.

First published 2003 by Macmillan Children's Books
a division of Macmillan Publishers Limited
20 New Wharf Road, London N1 9RR
Basingstoke and Oxford
www.panmacmillan.com

Associated companies throughout the world

ISBN 0 333 96114 5

1 3 5 7 9 8 6 4 2

A CIP catalogue record for this book is available from
the British Library.

Typeset by Macmillan Children's Books
Printed and bound in Great Britain by Mackays of Chatham plc, Kent

Contents

Boy on the Beach

Walking the dunes
Behind the strand,
I saw a boy alone
On wide, wet sand.
A stillness held him
As he faced the tide,
Slowly raised his arms
Then spread them wide;
Stayed so for a minute
Then breaking the spell,
Wrote large on the sand
With a stone or shell.
Walking on through marram grass
I soon could see:
He'd simply written
I AM ME.

Eric Finney
(England)

Don' Ride no Coconut Bough Down Dere

Papa face serious, him say 'dere's no way,
Ah want any o' yuh to go out an' play
An' mash up me yam hill dem down dey,
Specially wid unoo coconut bough.'

De hill so steep an' long an' slippery,
We could hear dat hill a-call out to we,
We could hear it a-say, 'come slide down me,
Yuh know yuh want to do it now.'

De yam vine dem twist roun' de hog plum tree,
Dem turn dem likkle face to we,
Dem say to Lainey, Bonnie an' to me,
'Memba whey yuh fada say.'

De coconut bough dem waitin' dere
Say, 'don' lissen to dem vine yuh year,
Yuh puppa really mean nex' year,
Him neva mean today.'

We fin' some bough, jus' what we need,
Head big an' solid, perfec' fe speed,
Me in de middle, Bonnie in de lead,
We jump pon we coconut bough dem.

An' den we all begin fe race,
De breeze like razor pon we face,
We feget 'bout goin' slow in case,
We break off Papa yam stem.

De t'ree o' we an de dog, Puppy,
Fly down de hill pass de pear tree,
Tear through de cocoa an' coffee,
We noh memba de yam no more.

Up de hill an' down agen,
Lean de bough into de ben'
We only see de yam vine dem when
We stop, 'bout half past four.

Dem lyin' lifeless pon de groun'
De hill dem flat, dem all mash down,
None o' we could meck a soun',
We didn' know wha' fe do.

De hill so steep an' long an' slippery,
We could hear dat hill a-call out to we,
We could hear it a-say, 'come slide down me,'
An we say, 'no, thank yuh!'

Valerie Bloom
(Jamaica/UK)

The Bridge

Poetry is a river
And solitude a bridge

Through writing
We cross it,
Through reading

We return.

Kaissar Afif
(Lebanon)

Poems to the Sun

All the cattle are resting in the fields,
The trees and the plants are growing,
The birds flutter above the marshes,
Their wings uplifted in adoration,
And all the sheep are dancing.
All winged things are flying,
They live when you have shone on them.

The boats sail upstream and downstream alike,
Every highway is open because you dawn.
The fish in the river leap up in front of you,
Your rays are in the middle of the great green sea.

Traditional
(Ancient Egypt)

The Moon Has Set

The Moon has set,
The Seven Stars have set as well:
It is the middle of the night,
The hour goes by,
And by myself I lie.

Sappho
(Greece)

This Afternoon

It's just the sort of afternoon
when ants take off and land on the moon
and conjure with such powerful spells
that – open your mouth – it'll rain caramels.

Tiitiäisen Satupuu
(Finland)

XVIII

Nothing makes me madder
Than to find I am not the first
Where I was blazing a trail.

Scarcely six years old
I heard there were machines
Travelling up the air and under water.

I resolved to invent a one
That would fly like a plane
Under earth.

Certain animals
Already do that
I was told.

Confound them!
Let small pox, great pox, goat pox, pox pox,
pix pox, pax pox, prax prox, prix prix prax,
pix pax pox, pox them!

Taban Lo Liyong
(Uganda)

By chance I walk . . .

By chance I walk into the western courtyard.
There in the shelter of the porch
A solitary orchid has flowered.
How quickly the news gets around
For already the bees are arriving.

Yüan Mei
(China)

Transformations

My little son enters
the room and says
'you are a vulture
I am a mouse'

I put away my book
wings and claws
grow out of me

their ominous shadows
race on the walls
I am a vulture
he is a mouse

'you are a wolf
I am a goat'
I walked around the table
and am a wolf
windowpanes gleam
like fangs
in the dark

while he runs to his mother
safe
his head hidden in the warmth of her dress

Tadeusz Różewicz
(Poland)

My Baby Has No Name Yet

My baby has no name yet;
like a new-born chick or puppy,
my baby is not named yet.

What numberless texts I examined
at dawn and night and evening over again!
But not one character did I find
which is lovely as the child.
Starry field of the sky,
or heap of pearls in the depth.
Where can the name be found, how can I?

My baby has no name yet;
like an unnamed bluebird or white flowers
from the farthest land for the first,
I have no name for this baby of ours.

Kim Nam-Jo
(Korea)

You Have Only One Mouth

You have got only one mouth
But two ears
So you talk once
And listen twice
You observe a lot, but talk very little,
You have got only one mouth but two hands
Therefore two for working and one for eating
food.

Kana kuwore kinu,
Indi maru nhawi
Nyi inera limu na aranja kawi
Ambuya mnu, indi amba kinu
Kana kuwore kinu, indi mawoka nhawi
Kouro, hawi uheryunda na limu
Iyeno kyumbo.

*The Chagga**
(Tanzania)

The Chagga are a group of people from Tanzania

Such Times

I walk across the playground. And all of a sudden
a six-year-old boy rushes to me
with wild strawberry cheeks.
In his hand he clutches a pop gun.
'Bang! Bang!' – he shoots at me.
Then he sticks the weapon in his pocket.
'Gotcha!' he says and runs off.

I notify the family. Friends.
I phone the police and report my death.
They spread their helpless hands.
'Such times' – they say.

Ewa Lipska
(Poland)

Forest and River

'I wish I were like you,'
Said the forest
  to the roaring river,
'Always travelling,
  always sightseeing;
Rushing towards the pure domain
  of the sea,
The kingdom or water;
Water,
The passionate, vigorous spirit
  of life,
The liquid turquoise of light
With eternal flow . . .

'But what am I?
Only a captive,
  chained to the earth.
In silence I grow old,
In silence I wither and die,
and before long
  nothing will remain of me
But a handful of ashes.'

'O forest, half-asleep, half-awake,'
Cried the river,
'I wish I were you,
enjoying a seclusion
        of living emerald,
And illuminated by moonlit nights;
Being a mirror
        reflecting the beauties
        of spring;
A shaded rendezvous for lovers.

'Your destiny, a new life
        every year;
My life, running away from myself
        all the time;
Running, running, running
        in bewilderment;
And what is my gain
Of all this meaningless journey?
Ah . . . never having a moment of calm.
        and rest!

'No one can ever know
    what the other feels;
Who does care to ask
    about a passer-by
If he really existed
Or was only a shadow?'

Now a passer-by
Aimlessly walking in the shade
Comes to ask himself,
'Who am I? a river? a forest?
Or both?
River and forest?
River and forest!'

Zhâleh Esfahâni
(Iran)

Amalkanti

Amalkanti is a friend of mine,
we were together at school.
He often came late to class
and never knew his lessons.
When asked to conjugate a verb,
he looked out of the window
in such puzzlement
that we all felt sorry for him.

Some of us wanted to be teachers,
some doctors, some lawyers.
Amalkanti didn't want to be any of these.
He wanted to be sunlight –
the timid sunlight of late afternoon,
when it stops raining
and the crows call again,
the sunlight that clings like a smile
to the leaves of the *jaam* and the *jaamrul*.

Some of us have become teachers,
some doctors, some lawyers.
Amalkanti couldn't become sunlight.
He works in a poorly lit room for a printer.
He drops in now and then to see me,
chats about this and that
over a cup of tea, then gets up to go.
I see him off at the door.
The one among us who's a teacher
could easily have become a doctor.
If the one who'd wanted to be a doctor
had become a lawyer,
it wouldn't have made much difference to him.
All of us got more or less what we wanted,
all except Amalkanti –
who used to think so much about sunlight
that he wanted to become sunlight.

Nirendranath Chakrabarti
(India)

The Wheel Around the World

If all the world's children
wanted to play holding hands
they could happily make
a wheel around the sea.

If all the world's children
wanted to play holding hands
they could be sailors
and build a bridge across the seas.

What a beautiful chorus we would make
singing around the earth
if all the humans in the world
wanted to dance holding hands!

Children's Song
(Mozambique)

Two Spanish Gypsy Lullabies

An angel of cinnamon
guards your cradle,
the head at the sun
the feet at the moon.

Under the laurels,
my daughter's cradle,
and when the moon rises
it calls her,
it calls her.

Anon.
(Spain)

South Wind

The days grow long, the mountains
Beautiful. The south wind blows
Over blossoming meadows.
Newly arrived swallows dart
Over the steaming marshes.
Ducks in pairs drowse on the warm sand.

Tu Fu
(China)

Mother Without a Husband

'My family reaches for bread.
My family reaches for milk.
My family reaches for water.
The milk just drawn from the cows
Is a trickle to dirty the jug.
The bread is a lump in my throat
And a crumbling of their faces.
I have no water to spare
For a mother's rightful tears.'

Meanwhile a poet standing by
Notes that 'Rain' rhymes with 'Grain',
And that he is not the one who is going to die.

Leo Aylen
(England)

Three

He remembers the faces
riding on the bus,
sweating on the subway,
floating on the ferry
reflected through shop windows,
and glowing through car windows.
And when he went to school
his class was full of faces,
serious faces, smiling faces,
dreaming faces, puzzled faces
trying hard to understand.
And after school out in the streets
he remembers faces coming
like a river down the hallway,
faces of so many colors
from mahogany to tangerine,
from chocolate dark to vanilla cream,
and hair that floated by
like dark cotton candy
and wavy gleaming hair
cut clean and tidy
and he collected these
faces and tucked them away
in the place where we keep
our dreams and daydreams.

Kwame Dawes   (USA)

John Anderson, My Jo

John Anderson my jo*, John,   *joy*
When we were first acquent,
Your locks were like the raven,
Your bonnie brow was brent;
But now your brow is beld, John,
Your locks are like the snow;
But blessings on your frosty pow*,   *head*
John Anderson, my jo.

John Anderson my jo, John,
We clamb* the hill thegither;   *climbed*
And mony a canty* day, John,   *merry*
We've had wi' ane anither:
Now we maun totter down, John,
And hand in hand we'll go,
And sleep thegither at the foot
John Anderson, my jo.

Robert Burns
(Scotland)

First Fig

My candle burns at both ends;
    It will not last the night;
But ah, my foes, and oh, my friends –
    It gives a lovely light!

Edna St Vincent Millay
(USA)

Mulga Bill's Bicycle

'Twas Mulga Bill, from Eaglehawk, that caught the
    cycling craze;
He turned away from the good old horse that served
    him many days;
He dressed himself in cycling clothes, resplendent to
    be seen;
He hurried off to town and bought a shining new
    machine;
And as he wheeled it through the door, with air of
    lordly pride,
The grinning shop assistant said, 'Excuse me, can
    you ride?'
'See here, young man,' said Mulga Bill, 'from Walgett to
    the sea,
From Conroy's Gap to Castlereagh, there's none can ride
    like me.
I'm good all round at everything, as everybody knows,
Although I'm not the one to talk – I hate a man
    that blows.
But riding is my special gift, my chiefest, sole delight;
Just ask a wild duck can it swim, a wild cat can it fight.
There's nothing clothed in hair or hide, or built of
    flesh or steel,
There's nothing walks or jumps, or runs, on axle, hoof,
    or wheel,

But what I'll sit, while hide will hold and girths and
straps are tight;
I'll ride this here two-wheeled concerned right straight
away at sight.'
'Twas Mulga Bill, from Eaglehawk, that sought his
own abode,
That perched above the Dead Man's Creek, beside the
mountain road.
He turned the cycle down the hill and mounted for
the fray,
But ere he'd gone a dozen yards it bolted clean away.
It left the track, and through the trees, just like a silver
streak,
It whistled down the awful slope towards the Dead
Man's Creek.

It shaved a stump by half an inch, it dodged a big
white-box:
The very wallaroos in fright went scrambling up
the rocks,
The wombats hiding in their caves dug deeper
underground,
But Mulga Bill, as white as chalk, sat tight to every
bound.
It struck a stone and gave a spring that cleared a fallen
tree,

It raced beside a precipice as close as close could be;
And then, as Mulga Bill let out one last despairing
    shriek,
It made a leap of twenty feet into the Dead Man's Creek.

'Twas Mulga Bill, from Eaglehawk, that slowly swam
    ashore:
He said, 'I've *never had* some narrer shaves and lively
    rides before;
I've rode a wild bull round a yard to win a
    five-pound bet,
But this was sure the derndest ride that I've
    encountered yet.
I'll give that two-wheeled outlaw best; it's shaken all
    my nerve
To feel it whistle through the air and plunge and buck
    and swerve.
It's safe at rest in Dead Man's Creek – we'll leave it
    lying still;
A horse's back is good enough henceforth for
    Mulga Bill.'

Banjo Patterson
(Australia)

Moving Country

Uncle Andrew's camera is on the table.
I am underneath the checked cover.
His shiny shoes walk out the door.
I grab his camera and run under
our house. Our house is on stilts.
All my secrets lie underneath.
My torch lights up my big blue box.
I run down the market, click
Mrs Joseph and her fish, click
my pal Frances, click the banana woman.

Suddenly we move to England.
Uncle Andrew takes our picture by the boat.
We wave and wave till he is a tiny dot.
At school they say, Where are you from?
Where are you from? Mimic my accent.
Rubber lips, they say. Chocolate Drop.
At night I twist my hair tight, tight.
Tell myself that my blue box is still there.
Write my friends a letter that starts,
'Here I am, my new school is brilliant.'

Jackie Kay
(Scotland)

After the Storm

After the rain has fallen
as if God had been dumping
gigantic buckets of water
I run outside
where puddles have formed
and splash around.

The world seems especially clean.
I twirl around.
I jump over rainbows.
I stomp real hard.
Mud splatters my clothes
in intricate designs.

Mother calls me in
Scolds me all the way to the bathroom.

After I have taken my bath
I peer through the window
loving this new world
washed clean by God's water.

Opal Palmer Adisa
(Jamaica/USA)

Haiku

A baby crab
Climbs up my leg –
Such clear water

Matsuo Basho
(Japan)

Haiku

At midnight
A distant door
Pulled shut.

Ozaki Hosai
(Japan)

Haiku

Winter downpour –
even the monkey
needs a raincoat.

Matsuo Basho
(Japan)

The Key of the Kingdom

This is the key of the kingdom:
In that kingdom is a city,
In that city is a town,
In that town there is a street,
In that street there winds a lane,
In that lane there is a yard,
In that yard there is a house,
In that house there waits a room,
In that room there is a bed,
On that bed there is a basket,
    A basket of flowers.

Flowers in the basket,
Basket on the bed,
Bed in the chamber,
Chamber in the house,
House in the weedy yard,
Yard in the winding lane,
Lane in the broad street,
Street in the high town,
Town in the city,
City in the kingdom:
    This is the key of the kingdom.

Anon.
(country unknown)

Hot Cake

Winter has come; fierce is the cold;
In the sharp morning air new-risen we meet.
Rheum freezes in the nose;
Frost hangs about the chin.
For hollow bellies, for chattering teeth
    and shivering knees
What better than hot cake?
Soft as the down of spring,
Whiter than autumn floss!
Dense and swift the stream
Rises, swells and spreads,
Fragrance flies through the air,
Is scattered far and wide,
Steals down along the wind and wets
The covetous mouth of passer-by.
Servants and grooms
Throw sidelong glances, munch the empty air.
They lick their lips who serve;
While lines of envious lackeys by the wall
Stand dryly swallowing.

Shu Hsi
(China)

Not a Very Mice Poem

Tom Cat, speak to me,
Sitting on your stone:
I think I'll go to Riga
With some mice from home:

Meat for the gentlemen
Roasted very nice!
Fur for the ladies' coats
Woven in a trice
And tails for the coachman's whips,
They'll pay a pretty price,
If I go to Riga
With my pretty pile of mice!

Traditional
(Latvian)

Harmony

The birds high above the town
Like notes upon a stave,
Composed in bolls of freckled brown
Along a sky of grey.

In measured, quavering sharps and flats
They write their treble tune,
While underneath, big minim cats
Await the breve-round moon.

How thrilling, though, the syncope
If ever there were more,
Than this sweet one-line melody:
A full orchestral score!

If hornbills, shrike and marabou
Joined sparrows on the wire,
Adding a different texture to
The soft, drab, round, brown choir;

If golden eagles, ducks and teal,
Parrots, geese and crane
Lent their sweet variety
To the mute evening refrain.

If bower birds and red macaws
And chuckling chickadees
Scattered around some brassy chords
And cage-birds changed the keys.

The birds roost all along the wire
Like notes beside a clef.
The skylark flies eight octaves higher
And evening holds its breath,
Awaiting the kind of harmony
Equal to writing a symphony
On the theme of sunset's fire.

Geraldine McCauchrean
(England)

Citizen of the World

when you are very small
maybe not quite born
your parents move
for some reason you may never
   understand they move
from their own town
from their own land
and you grow up in a place
that is never quite your home

and all your childhood people
with a smile or a fist say
you're not from here are you
and part of you says fiercely yes I am
and part of you feels no I'm not
I belong where my parents belonged

but when you go to their town, their country
people there also say
you're not from here are you
and part of you says no I'm not
and part of you feels fiercely yes I am

and so you grow up both and neither
and belong everywhere and nowhere much the same
both stronger and weaker for the lack of ground
able to fly but not to rest

and all over the world, though you feel alone
are millions like you, like a great flock of swallows
soaring or falling exhausted, wings beating the rhythm
of the wind that laughs at fences or frontiers,
whose home is itself, and the whole world it moves over.

Dave Calder
(Scotland)

Finding a Friend

I could not speak your language
I did not know your rules.
Everything felt foreign
to an alien at school.

Those days are long gone now,
though I thought they'd never end.
Now I have no problems
speaking English, making friends.

Dark and haunting memories
of loneliness and fear,
frustration and confusion
have begun to disappear.

But one thing I'll remember,
one thing will stay the same.
The moment that you smiled at me
and called me by my name.

Jane Clarke
(England)

Too Young to Know

I watch my mother's face.
I see the headlines, hear the radio.
The old men screw up the newspapers.
In town, the shutters are pulled down.

From my bed I hear people talking
late into the night. But when I dare
to go down and ask. When I dare
touch mother's hand, when I dare

to speak I am simply told:
Go away.
Go and play.
You're much too young to know.

Even the dog is hiding. He moves
from shadow to shadow with his head low.
I hug his neck and whisper in his ear:
Will there be a war?

He turns and licks my cheek.

Mandy Coe
(England)

My Feet are Killing Me

Some folks try to change the world
by marching armies overland
by taking elephants across the Alps
and building navies for all to see.

Rosa Parks sat down and said
'My feet are killing me.'

Some folks try to change the world
by parading on a pedestal
by saluting soldiers with their fluttering flags
and ranting and raving hysterically.

Rosa Parks sat down and said
'My feet are killing me.'

Some folks try to change the world
by poisoning your mind
by spreading words of hate
and making victims flee.

Rosa Parks sat down and said
'My feet are killing me.'

Sticks and stones
vilification
vile abuse
they were no use.
Why didn't they let her be?
Rosa Parks sighed and said
'My feet are killing me.'

*(The Montgomery bus boycott of 1955–56
in Alabama took place after Rosa Parks was
arrested following her refusal to give up her
seat to a white passenger.)*

John Clarke
(England)

Learning the Flowers

Along the lanes, down sunny hours,
That summer Granny taught me flowers:
Dog rose, foxglove, lady's smock,
Ox-eye daisy, townhall clock,
Billy's button, adder's meat,
Old man's beard and meadowsweet.
Sometimes I went to pick, but she
Smiled and said gently, 'Let them be.'
Sticky Willy, bugle, pansy,
Yellow rattle, harebell, tansy,
Silverweed and tormentil:
She taught me and I know them still.

Eric Finney
(England)

One Tree

one tree
so many leaves
one tree

one river
so many creeks
all are going to one sea

one head
so many thoughts
thoughts among which one good one
must be

one god
so many ways of worshipping
but one father

one Surinam
so many hair types
so many skin colours
so many tongues
one people

Dobru Ravales
(Surinam)

The Plough

I clench my fist
and bury the plough in the earth.
For years and years I have worked
no wonder I am worn out.

Butterflies are flying,
crickets are singing,
my skin gets darker and darker
and the sun glares, glares and glares.
Sweat furrows me,
I make furrows in the earth
on and on.

I hold fast to hope
when I think of my other star.
'It is never too late,' she tells me,
'The dove will fly one day.'

Butterflies are flying,
crickets are singing,
my skin gets darker and darker
and the sun glares, glares and glares.
And in the evening going home
in the sky I see a star.
'It is never too late,' she tells me,
'The dove will fly one day.'
As tight as a yoke
my fist is full of hope
because everything will change.

Victor Jara
(Chile)

When You Look at a Painting

When you look at a painting
let the dancing begin.
Move eyes round the frame
both gilded and plain,
then let the light take you in
to all that's within.

When you look at a painting
just don't stand and stare.
Let your eyes hold the waists
of the colours and the shapes,
let your eyes keep step
with the moods and the shades.

When you look at a painting
Let the dancing begin.
Let the rhythm unlock
the way your body rocks.
Don't be shy, get your eyes jumping.
Surprise the dancefloor of the painting.

Grace Nichols
(Guyana)

A Shell Awakening from Sleep

The soul is a straight line
said the second mathematician.
An arrow that pierces deep.

The soul is a triangle
said the third mathematician
The unity of three in one.

The soul is a square
said the fourth mathematician.
Each side a benediction.

The soul is a circle
said the fifth mathematician.
A wheel forever turning.

How shall I put it?
said the last mathematician.
The soul is anybody's guess.

But I'd like to suggest
the soul is an egg
holding itself within itself.

John Agard
(Guyana)

To everything there is a season,
A time for every purpose under heaven:

A time to be born,
>And a time to die;

A time to plant,
>And a time to pluck what is planted:

A time to kill,
>And a time to heal;

A time to break down,
>And a time to build up;

A time to weep,
>And a time to laugh;

A time to mourn,
>And a time to dance;

A time to cast away stones,
>And a time to gather stones;

A time to embrace,
>And a time to refrain from embracing;

A time to gain,
>And a time to lose;

A time to keep,
>And a time to throw away;

A time to tear,
>And a time to sew;

A time to keep silence,
    And a time to speak;
A time to love,
    And a time to hate;
A time of war,
    And a time of peace.

Ecclesiastes 3:1-8
(The Bible)

Alba

Dawn breaking as I woke,
With the white sweat of the dew
On the green, new grass.
I walked in the cold, quiet as
If it were the world beginning;
Peeling and eating a chilled tangerine.
I may have many sorrows,
Dawn is not one of them.

Derek Walcott
(St Lucia)

In Yung-Yang

I was a child in Yung-Yang,
A little child I waved farewell.
After long years again I dwell
In world-forgotten Yung-Yang.
Yet I recall my play-time,
And in my dreams I see
The little ghosts of May-time
Waving farewell to me.

My father's house in Yung-Yang
Has fallen upon evil days.
No kinsmen o'er the crooked ways
Hail me as once in Yung-Yang.
No longer stands the old Moot-hall,
Gone is the market from the town;
The very hills have tumbled down
And stoned the valleys in their fall.

Only the waters of the Chi'in and Wei
Roll green and changeless as in days gone by.

Yet I recall my play-time,
and in my dreams I see
The little ghosts of May-time
Waving farewell to me.

Po Chu-I
(China)

The Naming Ceremony

Her name sounds like water, like waves on the sea,
like a summer breeze in the tallest tree.
Ashanti, Ashanti, Ashanti.

Her dad is black, her mum is white.
They said, 'Please wear something bright.'
For Ashanti, Ashanti, Ashanti.

We made a great circle under the sun.
Some poems were read, some songs were sung.
To Ashanti, Ashanti, Ashanti.

We rattled our shakers, made music with bells.
A storyteller told tales, cast good African spells.
Over Ashanti, Ashanti, Ashanti.

They blessed her, sprinkling her face with water,
said a prayer of thanks for their little daughter.
Our Ashanti, Ashanti, Ashanti.

Her black grandfather then planted a tree.
Her white grandma held her up for all to see.
Ashanti, Ashanti, Ashanti.

She was passed like a parcel in a party game,
as each whispered in turn her beautiful name.
Ashanti, Ashanti, Ashanti.

Moira Andrew
(England)

A Tree Toad Loved a She-toad

A tree toad loved a she-toad
That lived up in a tree.
She was a three-toed tree toad,
But a two-toed toad was he.
The two-toed toad tried to win
The she-toad's friendly nod,
For the two-toed toad loved the ground
On which the three-toed toad trod.
But no matter how the two-toed tree toad tried,
He could not please her whim.
In her tree-toad bower,
With her three-toed power,
The she-toad vetoed him.

Anon.
(country unknown)

The Sprat and the Jackfish

'Who cares if it's fair?'
the jackfish said,
flicking its fin,
flashing its head.

'It's nothing to me
that you found it first;
it's mine to keep
though you cry till you burst.'

The small sprat flapped
its silver tail
and thought, 'I wish
I were a whale.

I'd swallow this jackfish
with one gulp;
its body I would
turn to pulp.

Because you're just that much
bigger than me,
you think you're the ruler
of the sea!

Well, take my worm
it's yours all right –
in this unfair world
it's might that's right.'

'It's a juicy worm!'
the jackfish said,
flicking its fin,
flashing its head.

Then, choking and twisting,
tormented, it sped
along an invisible
line overhead . . .

But the sprat did not see
as it went on its way
'It's an unfair world,'
was all it could say.

Grace Walker Gordon
(Jamaica)

Minstrel's Song

There are, some people say, no riches in the
  bush.
But look at an anthill:
It has a helmet providing shelter from rain.
See that beetle:
His coat does not go round him
And yet it has three buttons.
A bird which lives there in the bush
Has a wooden house:
Who is the carpenter?
This bush cow wears boots
Like those of a soldier;
That baboon has a black coat
Like a policeman;
And the kingfisher has a silk gown.
Why, then, do some people say
There are no riches in the bush?

The Mende*
(Sierra Leone)

*The Mende are a group of people from Sierra Leone

But I Heard the Drops

My father had a reservoir
of tears.
They trickled down
unseen.
But I heard the drops
drip
from his voice
like drops
from a loosened tap.
For thirty years
I heard them.

Sharif S. Elmusa
(Lebanon)

Hunt

I never have been in pursuit of words.
All I ever looked for
Was traces of their passage
Like the long silver haul
Of sunlight sweeping the grass
Or moonblinds drawn on the sea.

The shadows of words
Are what I hunted –
And hunting these is a skill
Best learned from the elders.
The elders know
That nothing is more precious
In a word
Than the shadow it casts
And words with no shadows to cast
Have lost their word-souls.

Ana Blandiana
(Romania)

And Then What?

The old man sat down on the bench.
His grey hair told his age.
The student who'd been there before
Sniffed once, and turned a page.
The old man gently touched his sleeve
'Excuse me, son,' said he.
The student turned his head, surprised,
What could the trouble be?
'Why study so,' the old man asked.
'Will you tell this to me?'
The youth replied 'So I may go
To university,'
'And after you have studied there,'
The old man asked, 'Then what?'
'Then I will find a well-paid job
With the degree I've got.'
The old man sighed. 'What after that?'
He asked with quivering voice.
'Then I will set up homestead with
The lady of my choice.'
'And after this,' the old man probed,
'What will life hold for thee?'
'W-why then,' replied the shaken youth,
'I'll raise a family.'
'And when they've all grown up and gone

What will be left for you?'
'I shall grow old, my wife and I,
Yes that is what we'll do.'
'I know all this,' the old man said,
'This was my tale as well;
But after you've grown old, my son,
What will you do, pray tell?'
'Why then I'll die,' the student quipped
'When I'm three score and ten,'
'And after that,' the old man cried,
'And after death, WHAT THEN?'

G. K. Sammy
(Trinidad)

No Easy Task, Son

My son,
Stop gazing at me
And walk straight ahead;

I know
There is no road ahead
But open your eyes
And walk through
That fog of reality.

Keep running my son
Keep running, for into the unknown
You may stumble upon your
Fortune of happiness.

Ignore the mutilated bodies
My son,
Ignore the easy pleasures
That appear and disappear
Like bubbles in a stormy sea;

Open your ears wide
And hear the message
Of the whispering voices
Open your eyes and avoid the ditches,
Son,
Being alive is no easy task.

Everett Standa
(Kenya)

Swing Low, Sweet Chariot

I ain't never been to heaven but I been told,
Comin' for to carry me home,
That the streets in heaven are paved with gold,
Comin' for to carry me home.

    Swing low, sweet chariot,
    Comin' for to carry me home,
    Swing low, sweet chariot,
    Comin' for to carry me home.

That ain't all, I got more besides –
I been to the river an' I been baptize'.

Lemme tell you what's a matter o' fact,
If you ever leave the devil, you never go back.

You see them sisters dress so fine?
Well, they ain't got Jesus on their mind.

If salvation was a thing money could buy,
Then the rich would live an' the poor would die.

But I'm so glad God fix it so,
That the rich must die just as well as the poor!

Anon.
(USA)

Ezekiel Saw the Wheel

Ezek'el saw the wheel
'Way up in the middle o' the air,
Ezek'el saw the wheel
'Way up in the middle o' the air.

The big wheel moved by Faith,
The little wheel moved by the Grace of God,
A wheel in a wheel,
'Way up in the middle o' the air.

Jes' let me tell you what a hypocrite'll do,
'Way up in the middle o' the air,
He'll talk about me an' he'll talk about you!
'Way up in the middle o' the air.

Ezek'el saw the wheel
'Way up in the middle o' the air,
Ezek'el saw the wheel
'Way up in the middle o' the air.

The big wheel moved by Faith,
The little wheel moved by the Grace of God,
A wheel in a wheel,
'Way up in the middle o' the air.

Watch out my sister how you walk on the cross,
'Way up in the middle o' the air,
Your foot might slip and your soul get lost!
'Way up in the middle o' the air.

Ezek'el saw the wheel
'Way up in the middle o' the air,
Ezek'el saw the wheel
'Way up in the middle o' the air.

The big wheel moved by Faith,
The little wheel moved by the Grace of God,
A wheel in a wheel,
'Way up in the middle o' the air.

You say the Lord has set you free,
'Way up in the middle o' the air.
Why don't you let your neighbors be!
'Way up in the middle o' the air.

Ezek'el saw the wheel
'Way up in the middle o' the air,
Ezek'el saw the wheel
'Way up in the middle o' the air.

The big wheel moved by Faith,
The little wheel moved by the Grace of God,
A wheel in a wheel,
'Way up in the middle o' the air.

Anon.
(USA)

The Two Roots

A pair of pine roots, old and dark,
make conversation in the park.

The whispers where the top leaves grow
are echoed in the roots below.

An aged squirrel sitting there
is knitting stockings for the pair.

The one says: squeak. The other: squawk.
That is enough for one day's talk.

Christian Morgenstern
(Germany)

Fern Hill

Now as I was young and easy under the apple boughs
About the lilting house and happy as the grass was green,
> The night above the dingle starry,
>> Time let me hail and climb
>> Golden in the heydays of his eyes,
And honoured among wagons I was prince of the apple
  towns
And once below a time I lordly had the trees and leaves
> Trail with daisies and barley
>> Down the rivers of the windfall light.

As I was green and carefree, famous among the barns
About the happy yard and singing as the farm was home,
> In the sun that is young once only,
>> Time let me play and be
>> Golden in the mercy of his means,
And green and golden I was huntsman and herdsman, the
  calves.
Sang to my horn, the foxes on the hills barked clear and
  cold.
> And the sabbath rang slowly
>> In the pebbles of the holy streams.

All the sun long it was running, it was lovely, the hay
Fields high as the house, the tunes from the chimneys, it
   was air
      And playing, lovely and watery
         And fire green as grass.
      And nightly under the simple stars
As I rode to sleep the owls were bearing the farm away,
All the moon long I heard, blessed among stables, the
   nightjars
      Flying with the ricks, and the horses
      Flashing into the dark.

And then to awake, and the farm, like a wanderer white
With the dew, come back, the cock on his shoulder: it
   was all
      Shining, it was Adam and maiden,
         The sky gathered again
      And the sun grew round that very day.
So it must have been after the birth of the simple light
In the first, spinning place, the spellbound horses walking
   warm
      Out of the whinnying green stable
         On to the fields of praise.

And honoured among foxes and pheasants by the gay
    house
Under the new made clouds and happy as the heart was
    long,
        In the sun born over and over,
            I ran my heedless ways,
My wishes raced through the house high hay
And nothing I cared, at my sky blue trades, that time
    allows
In all his tuneful turning so few and such morning songs
        Before the children green and golden
            Follow him out of grace,

Nothing I cared, in the lamb white days, that time would
    take me
Up to the swallow thronged loft by the shadow of my hand,
        In the moon that is always rising,
            Nor that riding to sleep
        I should hear him fly with the high fields
And wake to the farm forever fled from the childless land.
Oh as I was young and easy in the mercy of his means,
        Time held me green and dying
            Though I sang in my chains like the sea.

Dylan Thomas
(Wales)

Walnut

The pale green coat
of the walnut has split,
small wonder, since spring
he has been wearing it.

Autumn could mend it
with gossamer thread
but would stitches hold
for the winter ahead?

The wind gathers strength
over field and road
and shakes the walnut
out of his coat.

István Pákolitz
(Hungary)

A Helping Hand

We gave a helping hand to grass –
    and it turned into corn.
We gave a helping hand to fire –
    and it turned into a rocket.
Hesitatingly,
cautiously,
we give a helping hand
to people,
to some people . . .

Miroslav Holub
(the former Czechoslovakia)

My House

I had a house for seven years:
I must have climbed the stair
Five thousand times; and every day
Locked and unlocked the door.
It watched me clean my teeth, and wash
My face, and brush my hair.

And then I went away, and so
Put up my house to let,
'Just think,' I said, 'of all the lovely
Money I will get.'
A stranger known as Mr Jones
Came to live in it.

A year went by; and I came back,
And all I brought was new:
New shoes, new suit, new suitcase too,
New plans for what I'd do.
But when I put my latchkey in,
My house said, 'Who are you?'

Laurence Lerner
(England)

Square Peg

I was a knight of the Round Table –
I killed dragons for my livelihood.

I was offered voluntary redundancy
for today's dragons have all been given knighthoods.

Debjani Chatterjee
(India)

Sometimes

in
all
the
rush
and
hurry
of
our
lives
we
need
so
much
just
now
and
then
to
find
an

island

Kenneth C. Steven
(Scotland)

Touching

This is a song
about touch and touching.
You touch me – a way of feeling.
I touch you – a way of understanding.
We are touched
by a film or a book.
We are touched
when a stranger is kind.
How can we live
without touching and being touched?

There is a healing touch,
it makes the sick whole again.
Let's keep in touch
we say to a friend who's going away.
To have the right touch
means to know how it's done.
Touching is an art,
it's the movement
to and from the heart.

Some are easily touched.
Some are hard to touch.
You are often touched.
I am often touched.

Nissim Ezekiel
(Pakistan)

A Nest Full of Stars

Only chance made me come and find
my hen, stepping from her hidden
nest, in our kitchen garden.

In her clever secret place, her tenth
egg, still warm, had just been dropped.

Not sure of what to do, I picked up
every egg, counting them, then put them
down again. *All were mine.*

All swept me away and back.
I blinked, I saw: a whole hand
of ripe bananas, nesting.

I blinked, I saw: a basketful
of ripe oranges, nesting.

I blinked, I saw: a trayful
of ripe naseberries, nesting.

I blinked, I saw: an open bagful
of ripe mangoes, nesting.

I blinked, I saw:
a mighty nest full of stars.

James Berry
(Jamaica)

In Praise of Noses

Not exactly ornamental
even when quite straight,
these funny, two-holed things!

But think:
if they faced upwards
they'd blow hats off

when once squeezed
and fill with rain
when it poured.

If sideways,
what objects of derision
snuff-takers would be!

Now all that a sneeze merits
is a 'God bless'.

God bless indeed, sweet nose,
warming, filtering,

humidifying the air as I breathe,
you do a marvellous job!

Prabhu S. Guptara
(India/UK)

Only the Moon

When I was a child I thought
the new moon was a cradle
The full moon was granny's round face.

The new moon was a banana
The full moon was a big cake.

When I was a child
I never saw the moon
I only saw what I wanted to see.

And now I see the moon
It's the moon
Only the moon, and nothing but the moon.

Wong May
(Singapore)

My House

I have built my house
Without sand, without water
My mother's heart
Forms a great wall
My father's arms
The floor and the roof
My sister's laughter
The doors and the windows
My brother's eyes
Light up the house
My home feels good
My home is sweet

Annette Mbaye d'Erneville
(Senegal)

How to Paint the Portrait of a Bird

First paint a cage
with an open door
then paint
something pretty
something simple
something fine
something useful
for the bird
next place the canvas against a tree
in a garden
in a wood
or in a forest
hide behind the tree
without speaking
without moving . . .
Sometimes the bird comes quickly
but it can also take many years
before making up its mind
Don't be discouraged
wait
wait if necessary for years
the quickness or the slowness of the coming
of the bird having no relation
to the success of the picture.
When the bird comes
if it comes

observe the deepest silence
wait for the bird to enter the cage
and when it has entered
gently close the door with the paintbrush
then
one by one paint out all the bars
taking care not to touch one feather of the bird
Next make a portrait of the tree
choosing the finest of its branches
for the bird
paint also the green leaves and the freshness of the wind
dust in the sun
and the sound of the insects in the summer grass
and wait for the bird to decide to sing.
If the bird does not sing
it is a bad sign
a sign that the picture is bad
but if it sings it is a good sign
a sign that you are already to sign
so then you pluck very gently
one of the quills of the bird
and you write your name in the corner of the picture.

Jacques Prévert
(France)

Midsummer, Tobago

Broad sun-stoned beaches.

White heat.
A green river.

A bridge,
scorched yellow palms

from the summer-sleeping house
drowsing through August.

Days I have held,
days I have lost,

days that outgrow, like daughters,
my harbouring arms.

Derek Walcott
(St Lucia)

The Most Beautiful Sound in the World?

Water
in the dry season
running out from a communal tap.

Kadija Sesay
(UK)

A Huggle

A huggle
is more than a snuggle.
It's different from a cuddle.

A snuggle has got to be right,
a cuddle is sometimes tight
squeezing away softness;

but a huggle
is soft and warm,
full of arms.

It's even better
than treacle toffee.

John Lyons
(England)

The King and the Wind

'Come,' said the King,
'come and all these I shall give you:

> a moated castle with knights to protect you,
> a banqueting hall with servants to feed you,
> a treasure chest with silver to please you.'

'Stay,' said the Wind,
'stay and all these shall I give you:

> a sky with clouds ever changing,
> a mountain with glens ever singing,
> a shore with waves ever dancing.'

'Come,' said the King; 'Stay,' said the Wind.

John Rice
(Scotland)

This poem comes from the Gaelic saying:
'Thugainn,' ars' an Righ; 'Fuirich,' ars' a' ghaoth.

Heather

Heather wipes the young ones' faces,
Tucks them into bed,
Ignores the thoughts of better places
Sneaking through her head.

Whether it be rain in springtime
Or hot summer sun,
There's war to fight with dust and grime
And errands to be run.

Leather split in shoes and sandals
Must be patched. The door
Fresh graffitied by the vandals
Must be cleaned once more.

Heather, gently bathes her mother,
Feeds her, combs her hair,
Thoughts of school she tries to smother,
Perhaps she'll go next year.

Valerie Bloom
(Jamaica/UK)

Coal Tip Mountain

Like a shadow
cast across the hills by a century
of mining

slag-heap mountain –
what was left to us
and miners' dark and crackly laughter
out of dust-corrupted lungs
with memories of good-old-time-ing.

'Aye boyo they were the days, they were,
God knows what we've come to now . . .'

And we turned from their gilded lying
and looked at the mine shaft ruins,
the drunks outside the pubs,
the empty chapels . . .
And we knew then surely
that the valley was on the edge
of dying.

Stephen Bowkett
(Wales)

After Snow

Just a few footprints in the snow:
Yours perhaps? I wouldn't know.
I'm certain that they are not mine.
First-footing in new snow is fine,
But waking to that dazzling white
After secret snow at night,
I'd wonder at a world new-minted
And leave perfection quite unprinted.

Eric Finney
(England)

CHRISTMAS ACROSS
Great Britain – Christmas Eve

Tonight the silver moon shivers,
white frost glitters on hills,

children sing round a Christmas tree
that glints in its tinsel frills.

They munch on mince pies by the fire
watched by a *Great Bear in the sky.

Each window's a stage – as the curtains close
Christmas Eve must say, 'Goodbye'.

Australia – Christmas Day

Today the golden sun shimmers,
orange dust covers the town,

children sing round a Christmas bush
that glows in its red-leaf gown.

They picnic on barbecued turkey,
watch stars draw an **Archer's bow

that quivers, 'Goodnight' in an inky sky.
Christmas Day, it's time to go.

*Great Bear constellation is seen only from the Northern
Hemisphere

**Archer constellation is seen only from the Southern
Hemisphere

Gina Douthwaite
(England)

Dream Variations

To fling my arms wide
In some place of the sun,
To whirl and to dance
Till the white day is done.
Then rest at cool evening
Beneath a tall tree
While night comes on gently,
    Dark like me –
That's my dream!

To fling my arms wide
In the face of the sun,
Dance! Whirl! Whirl!
Till the quick day is done.
Rest at pale evening . . .
A tall, slim tree . . .
Night coming tenderly
Black like me.

Langston Hughes
(USA)

America's Gate (Ellis Island)

'I'm bringing something beautiful to America.' (Girl, 10 years)

If I miss my name
    then I might be forever knocking
        on America's gate.
If I lose my ticket and miss my turn
    I may never learn the lie of this land.
For all that I've planned
    is tied up in this trip,
all that I own
    is packed up in this bag.
And there isn't much money
    but there's gifts I can bring.
And I'm bringing them all to America,
I'm bringing them all from home.
Not my mother's rings
    or my party dress,
not my father's watch
    or my lacy shawl,
just the moon on my shoulder,
    a voice that can sing,
feet that can dance
    and a pipe that I play.
And I'm playing now for America,
    and I'm hoping that someone will hear.
Then perhaps I won't be forever knocking
    on America's gate.

Brian Moses　　　　　　　　　　　(England)

I Hear America Singing

I hear America singing, the varied carols I hear,
   Those of mechanics, each one singing his
     as it should be blithe and strong,
       The carpenter singing his
        as he measures
          his plank or beam,

The mason singing his
  as he makes ready for work,
    or leaves off work,
The boatman singing what
     belongs to him in his boat,
   the deckhand singing on the steamboat deck,
The shoemaker singing as he sits
  on his bench, the hatter
   singing as he stands,

The wood-cutter's song,
  the ploughboy's on his way in the morning,
    or at noon intermission or at sundown,
     the delicious singing of the mother,
      or of the young wife at work,
       or of the girl sewing or washing,

Each singing what belongs to him
   or her and to no one else,
The day what belongs to the day –
   at night the party of young fellows, robust, friendly,
Singing with open mouths their strong melodious songs.

Walt Whitman
(USA)

Since You Went Away

Seems like to me, de stars don't shine so bright,
Seems like to me de sun done loss his light,
Seems like to me der's nothin' goin' right,
Since you went away.

Seems like to me de sky ain't half so blue,
Seems like to me dat everything wants you,
Seems like to me I don't know what to do,
Since you went away.

Seems like to me dat everything is wrong,
Seems like to me de day's jes twice as long,
Seems like to me de bird's forgot his song
Since you went away.

Seems like to me I jes can't help but sigh,
Seems like to me ma throat keeps getting dry,
Seems like to me a tear stays in ma eye,
Since you went away.

James Weldon Johnson
(USA)

And Now

It's a *rum-*
Ba band another *rum-*
Ba band a never *slum-*
Ba band there's any *num-*
Ba of *rum-*
Ba bands
      Shicker-shicker-shicker,
Turn on the radio,
Mammoth set or midget,
All you'll ever get
Is the everlasting fidget
Of a *rum-*
Ba band another *rum-*
Ba band a pluck and *strum-*
Ba band with a
Shicker-shicker-shicker-shicker
Shee shicker-shick and a
Ticker-ticker-ticker-ticker
Tee Ticker-tick and a
Boom and a nobble and a clang
And a bang
And a chatter and a natter
Let it clatter
Let it shatter
Let it spatter
Doesn't matter

Getting flatter.
Turn on the radio,
Mammoth set or midget,
All you seem to get
Is the orchestrated fidget
Of a *rum-*
Ba band another *rum-*
Ba band, there's any *num*-BA . . .
To play the *rum*-BA . . .
Can't someone have the rumba banned?
     (Shicker-shick)

J. B. Boothroyd
(England)

I Shall Return

I shall return again. I shall return
To laugh and love and watch with wonder eyes
At golden noon the forest fires burn,
Wafting their blue-black smoke to sapphire skies,
I shall return to loiter by the streams
That bathe the brown blades of the bending grasses,
And realize once more my thousand dreams
Of waters rushing down the mountain passes.
I shall return to hear the fiddle and fife
Of village dances, dear delicious tunes
That stir the hidden depths of native life,
Stray melodies of dim-remembered runes.
I shall return. I shall return again
To ease my mind of long, long years of pain.

Claude McKay
(Jamaica)

Hanukkah

Hanukkah is the story
of the Maccabees; father
and brothers, brave and strong.

Hanukkah is the miracle
of one day's oil
that burned for eight days long.

Hanukkah is candle flames
blooming and glowing
through eight dark winter nights.

Hannukah is *latkes* and doughnuts
and singing songs together
gathered around the flickering lights.

Hanukkah is gifts with smiles
and sharing out sweets or nuts
for the *dreydel* game.

Hanukkah is remembering
and giving thanks
every year the same.

Penny Kent
(England)

Up on the Roof

Up on the roof of a church
was a small, blond boy
and a black and white kitten.

Down below, the priest
was praying aloud,
pleading with God,

asking him to keep
this small boy from falling
down from his church.

He couldn't phone the mother
as he didn't know her,
and cats all looked the same.

When the verger appeared
with a telescopic ladder
the priest closed his eyes

and, gripping his rosary,
he prayed in the dark until
the verger began to climb.

The boy was on his feet now
calling the kitten
who refused to move.

'Sit down,' begged the priest,
in an almost whisper
so as not to alarm the boy

who paid no attention,
walking over the slates
as if on the pavement

or as if he had wings –
with the sun in his hair
he looked like an angel.

When the verger's bald head
rose above the drainpipe
the boy had the kitten

and was walking back,
along the ridge
with a beatific smile.

Matthew Sweeney
(Ireland)

The Lesson

'Your father's gone,' my bald headmaster said.
His shiny dome and brown tobacco jar
Splintered at once in tears. It wasn't grief.
I cried for knowledge which was bitterer
Than any grief. For there and then I knew
That grief has uses—that a father dead
Could bind the bully's fist a week or two;
And then I cried for shame, then for relief.

I was a month past ten when I learnt this:
I still remember how the noise was stilled
In school-assembly when my grief came in.
Some goldfish in a bowl quietly sculled
Around their shining prison on its shelf.
They were indifferent. All the other eyes
Were turned towards me. Somewhere in myself
Pride, like a goldfish, flashed a sudden fin.

Edward Lucie-Smith
(Jamaica)

Village Life

So boring, so dull and
isolated,
Very quiet, you feel
uneasy
Meeting the same old
faces.
When you ask, 'Yu go
we?'
They'll nod and say,
'Mi go wok'.
The elders talking and
smoking
At the corner of the
singsing place,
Ignoring you.

You'll feel as a lost ship
on the ocean.
Life is so boring, so dull
and isolated.
One thing I wish for . . .
The bright lights.

Johannes Korop
(New Guinea)

For a Little Love

For a little love, I would go to the end of the world;
I would go with my head bare and feet unshod,
I would go through ice, but in my soul forever May,
I would go through the storm, but still hear the
  blackbird sing,
I would go through the desert, and have pearls of dew
  in my heart.
For a little love, I would go to the end of the world,
Like the one, who sings at the door and begs.

Jaroslav Vrchlicky
(the former Czechoslovakia)

I Shall Sing

I shall create
out of the darkness of my jail
my dawn
out of the jaws of hatred
my destiny.
I shall sing
the wind
the sun
the flowers
the spring.
I shall sing
in spite of fences
in spite of jailers
in spite of hatred.

Fouzi El-Asmar
(Palestine)

Peace

Peace is the odour of food in the evening,
when the halting of a car in the street is not fear,
when a knock on the door means a friend

Peace is a glass of warm milk
and a book in front of the child who awakens

Yannis Ritsos
(Greece)

South to North; 1965

I was born South of the river
down in the delta, beyond the bayou
lived in the swamps just off the High Street
London alligators snapping my ankles.

It was Bromley, Beckenham, Penge, Crystal Palace
where the kids said *wotcha*, ate bits of *cike*,
the land my father walked as a boy
the land his father walked before him.

I was rooted there, stuck in the clay
until we drove North, moved to Yorkshire
a land of cobbles, coal pits and coke works
forges and steel, fires in the sky.

Where you walked through fields around your village
didn't need three bus-rides to see a farm.

It was Mexbrough, Barnsley, Sprotborough, Goldthorpe
I was deafened by words, my tongue struck dumb
gobsmacked by a language I couldn't speak in.

Ayop sithee, it's semmers nowt
What's tha got in thi snap, chaze else paze?
Who does tha supoort, Owls else Blades?
Dun't thee tha me, thee tha thi sen
Tha's a rate un thee, giz a spice?

Cheese and peas, sweets and football
I rolled in a richness of newfound vowels
words that dazed, dazzled and danced
out loud in my head until it all made sense
In this different country, far away
from where I was born, South of the river.

David Harmer
(England)

The Bells

I love them, I hear them,
just as I hear the sound of the wind,
the babbling of the fountain
or the bleating of the lamb.

Just as the birds do, so they too,
the moment there appears in the sky
the first gleam of dawn,
greet it with their echoes.

And in their tones, that linger
over the plains and hills,
there is something candid,
peaceful and endearing.

Should they become forever mute,
what sadness in the air and sky!
what silence in the churches!
what wonder among the dead!

Rosalia Castro
(Spain)

The Star Counters

I am tired.

   I contemplate
this town

   – a town like any other –
where I have lived for twenty years.

Nothing has changed.
   A child
   is uselessly counting the stars
on the next balcony.

     I also try . . .

But he is faster: I cannot
catch up with him;

     One, two, three, four,

five . . .

I cannot

catch up with him: One . . . two . . .
three . . .
   four . . .
     five . . .

Damaso Alonso
(Spain)

Grandpa and His Canary

My silver-bearded Grandpa
Chuckles like an old locust tree shaking loose
    its blooms.
Early every morning
He hangs his finely woven birdcage on a branch
and closely scrutinizes the little canary,
Still a baby, all golden and downy.
How Grandpa grins with glee.

Up, up
He lifts my stocky body up
For me to feed the bird a few grains
And coax it into sweet song.

Crack goes the branch,
The cage is broken,
The bird has flown,
Shattering Grandpa's perpetual delight.
He raises his cane as if wanting to hit me
But I can't tell him where the bird has gone.

Grandpa, clutching the mended cage,
Sets out with me to scour the woods.
A peep of clear crisp trilling notes
Leads us to our joyous find –
Upon a leafy branch
Perches our golden canary
It twitters:
I'm not going back with you,
I've built myself a fine sturdy nest.

Looking upward at the nest,
Frosty beard quivering and
Dropping like sweatbeads.
Is Grandpa crying or laughing?
Tapping my shoulder he wildly gestures:
Fly, oh fly away . . .

Shen Aiping
(China)

The Prayer of the Cat

Lord,
I am the cat,
It is not, exactly, that I have something to ask of You!
No –
I ask nothing of anyone –
but,
if You have by some chance, in some celestial barn,
a little white mouse,
or a saucer of milk,
I know someone who would relish them.
Wouldn't You like some day
to put a curse on the whole race of dogs?
If so I should say,

Amen

Carmen Bernos de Gasztold
(France)

While the Leaves Were Still Green

While the leaves were still green,
We ate marmalade and bread,
But when the winter comes again,
Just walnuts and eggs painted yellow and red!

Traditional
(the former Yugoslavia)

Blackberry-Picking

FOR PHILIP HOBSBAUM

Late August, given heavy rain and sun
For a full week, the blackberries would ripen.
At first, just one, a glossy purple clot
Among others, red, green, hard as a knot.
You ate that first one and its flesh was sweet
Like thickened wine: summer's blood was in it
Leaving stains upon the tongue and lust for
Picking. Then red ones inked up and that hunger
Sent us out with milk-cans, pea-tins, jam-pots
Where briars scratched and wet grass bleached our boots.
Round hayfields, cornfields and potato-drills
We trekked and picked until the cans were full,
Until the tinkling bottom had been covered
With green ones, and on top big dark blobs burned
Like a plate of eyes. Our hands were peppered
With thorn pricks, our palms sticky as Bluebeard's.

We hoarded the fresh berries in the byre.
But when the bath was filled we found a fur,
A rat-grey fungus, glutting on our cache.
The juice was stinking too. Once off the bush
The fruit fermented, the sweet flesh would turn sour.
I always felt like crying. It wasn't fair
That all the lovely canfuls smelt of rot.
Each year I hoped they'd keep, knew they would not.

Seamus Heaney   (Ireland)

The Hare's House

Underneath a clump of broom
Hare has built himself a home.
What a builder, what a home,
All around the cold winds roam.

He blocked the windows up with moss,
Barred the door with cones across,
What a palace for a hare,
You'll see all the world from there!

From above, the house is hid
With some bracken for a lid!
What a cosy nook! You'll not
Without a fur coat sleep a jot!

And in winter, while you drowse,
Snowstorm sneaks into the house,
And Jack Frost will get in too,
They will freeze you till you're blue!

If he's not to freeze up quite,
Hare must jump about all night!
What a hare! And what a home,
Underneath the clump of broom!

Maksim Tank
(Belarus)

The Grasshopper and the Ant

Grasshopper, having sung her song
    All summer long,
Was sadly unprovided-for
When the cold wind began to roar:
Not one least grub or fly
Had she remembered to put by.
Therefore she hastened to descant
On famine, to her neighbour Ant,
Begging the loan of a few grains
Of wheat to ease her hunger pains
Until the winter should be gone.
'You shall be paid,' said she, 'upon
My honour as an animal,
Both interest and principal.'
The Ant was not disposed to lend;
That liberal vice was not for her.
'What did you do all summer, friend?'
She asked the would-be borrower.
'So please your worship,' answered she,
'I sang and sang both night and day.'
'You sang? Indeed, that pleases me.
Then dance the wintertime away.'

Jean de la Fontaine
(France)

There Was an Indian

There was an Indian, who had known no change,
  Who strayed content along a sunlit beach
Gathering shells. He heard a sudden strange
  Commingled noise; looked up; and gasped for speech.
For in the bay, where nothing was before
  Moved on the sea, by magic, huge canoes.
With bellying cloths on poles, and not one oar,
  And fluttering coloured signs and clambering crews.
And he, in fear, this naked man alone,
  His fallen hands forgetting all their shells,
His lips gone pale, knelt low behind a stone,
  And stared, and saw, and did not understand,
Columbus's doom-burdened caravels
  Slant to the shore, and all their seamen land.

Sir John Squire
(England)

What Is Snow?

He knew all about heat,
This child from Australia.
He knew the searing sun
    of afternoon,
the touch of unrelenting
    yellow light.

He knew all about waves,
this child of mile-long beaches.
He knew the pounding sound
    of breaking surf,
the deep cool blueness
    of the ocean.

He had never known snow,
this child of daylong sunshine,
in picture books, yes, but
    not for real,
not the quiet whiteness of
    a winter's day.

He had never seen the magic
of white on white. Entranced,
he watched the whirling flakes,
    'Can I play?'
he asked, too impatient for gloves
    or woolly hat.

He had never known cold,
this child of the burning sun,
the biting cold of snowballs
    on bare hands.
Disillusioned, he stood in the snow
    and sobbed.

Moira Andrew
(England)

Long Division Lesson

Sunil was a quiet child.
No one spoke to him
And he spoke to no one.
Our words jangled around him
Like untuned radios,
While his words whispered secretly
Inside his head.
Only his eyes flashed friendly messages:
'I am not unhappy.'
'I am not afraid of you.'
'I am not completely confused.'

Day after day he watched
While the others talked,
Or dreamed,
Or drew cartoons.
Day after day I scratched pale numbers
On the ghost-grey board.

'Long division,' I said.
'Don't worry if you find it tricky.
Everyone finds it tricky.'
I found it tricky,
So I explained and scratched,
Explained and scratched,
Day after dusty day.

At the end of term,
To test myself,
I tested them.
Only Sunil wrote perfect answers
In perfect, neat rows,
So I rewarded him with the universal language
Of ticks and golden stars,
And he rewarded me with a kindly smile.

Long division lessons can teach us
More than we expect.
Sometimes, for instance,
Numbers speak very clearly
For themselves.
And sometimes even teachers
Are tempted to talk too much.

Clare Bevan
(England)

The Good Taste Estate

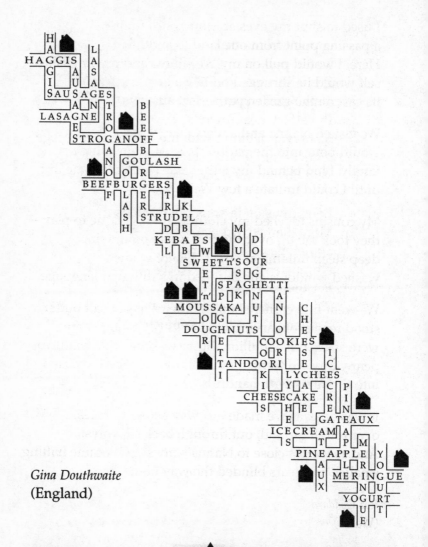

Gina Douthwaite
(England)

Visit

I used to shut my eyes at Monmouth tunnel,
a passing point from one land to another.
Here, I would pull on my Welshness and my English
self would be shrugged off like a creature leaving
its cast on the garden path.

We visited Nanna and a whole street of cousins
would pour into the parlour to see the Birmingham
family. I hid behind my father and wouldn't come out
until I could imitate a few Welsh words.

My cousins touched my clothes and urged me to play –
they took me up over the coal waste mountain,
deep steep unfamiliar streets where women
washed windows and laughed in a different language.

We went into corner shops: golden slabs of salt butter
stood ready for carving up, bricks of coal tar soap
were stacked like bullion. But it was the wide colourful
penny tray we wanted most and we skipped, dazzled
into the street with handfuls.

It was dusk as we made our way across terraces,
over rough ground, out through back slipways.
And as we got close to Nanna's my steps became halting,
smaller, and tears blinded the way home.

Roz Goddard
(Wales)

I Just Got Here

I've got a book, can't read the words
They fly and scatter like flocks of birds
Scared away by a sudden noise
But it doesn't worry the girls and boys
In my new class, they get things right
But I can't read much without a fight.

I'm trying to write but I can't spell
The letters jump and dance, can't tell
Which one comes second, last or first
No, at spelling I'm the worst
In the whole class, can't do it right
I can't spell at all without a fight.

I can't seem to talk or speak
And be understood, been here a week
I hear the sounds but I can't make sense
Of what they mean, can't climb the fence
See over their side and get it right
Can't communicate without a fight.

Back home of course in my own land
I was clever at school, could understand
Everything teachers said to me
I played with my friends, I could be
Just who I am, didn't have to fight
To speak and talk or read or write.

I get so lonely, angry, sad
Some days I think I'm going mad
Can't gossip, chatter, share a joke
Feel like I'm walking through thick smoke
But I'll work and work to get it right
I won't give up without a fight.

David Harmer
(England)

The Picnic in Jammu

Uncle Ayub swung me round and round
till the horizon became a rail
banked high upon the Himalayas.
The trees signalled me past. I whistled,
shut my eyes through tunnels of the air.
The family laughed, watching me puff
out my muscles, healthily aggressive.

This was late summer, before the snows
come to Kashmir, this was picnic time.

Then, uncoupling me from the sky, he
plunged me into the river, himself
a bough with me dangling at its end.
I went purple as a plum. He reared
back and lowered the branch of his arm
to Grandma who swallowed me with a kiss.
Laughter peeled away my goosepimples.

This was late summer, before the snows
come to Kashmir, this was picnic time.

After we'd eaten, he aimed grapes at
my mouth. I flung at him the shells of
pomegranates and ran off. He tracked
me down the riverbank. We battled,
melon-rind and apple-core our arms.
'You two!' Grandma cried. 'Stop fighting, you'll
tire yourselves to death!' We didn't listen.

This was late summer, before the snows
come to Kashmir and end children's games.

Zulfikar Ghose
(Pakistan)

Mela Menagerie

It was summertime,
the animals were having a mela.
  The elephants cooked
curried pumpkin with tikka masala,
  sun-shy frogs and mice
sheltered under the hood of a cobra,
  bears and cockatoos
swapped couplets in a mini mushaira,
  horses and camels
pranced and danced a fantastic bhangra,
  tigers took pot shot
at juicy papayas for one paisa,
  lions showed off paws
decorated with delicate henna,
  donkeys for a laugh
crowned a mule their day-long Maharaja,
  pelicans swallowed
swords with mango chutney and paratha,
  Sinbad's ship sailed in
on waves of dolphin abracadabra,
  monkeys built bridges
recalling how they once helped Prince Rama,
  while Ali Baba
and forty rooks acted out life's drama.
  It was summertime,
the animals were having a mela.

Debjani Chatterjee   (India)

This Is Just to Say

I have eaten
the plums
that were in
the icebox

and which
you were probably
saving
for breakfast

Forgive me
they were delicious
so sweet
and so cold

William Carlos Williams
(USA)

Lament of an Arawak Child

Once I played with the hummingbirds
and sang songs to the sea
I told my secrets to the waves
and they told theirs to me.

Now there are no more hummingbirds
the sea's songs are all sad
for strange men came and took this land
and plundered all we had.

They made my people into slaves
they worked us to the bone
they battered us and tortured us
and laughed to hear us groan.

Today we'll take a long canoe
and set sail on the sea
we'll steer our journey by the stars
and find a new country.

Pamela Mordecai
(Jamaica)

The Coromandel Fishers

Rise, brothers, rise; the waking skies pray to
the morning light,
The wind lies asleep in the arms of the dawn like
a child that has cried all night;
Come, let us gather our nets from the shore and set
our catamarans free
To capture the leaping wealth of the tide, for we
are the kings of the sea!

No longer delay, let us hasten away in the track of
the seagull's call,
The sea is our mother, the cloud is our brother, the
waves our comrades all,
What though we toss at the fall of the sun where
the hand of the sea-god drives?
He who holds the storm by the hair will hide in his
breast our lives.

Sweet is the shade of the coconut glade and the
scent of the mango grove,
And sweet are the sands at the fall of the moon
the sound of the voices we love;
But sweeter, O brothers, the kiss of the spray, and
the dance of the wild foam's glee;
Row, brothers, row, to the blue of the verge, where
the low sky mates with the sea.

Sarojini Naidu
(India)

Inside the Church

Every silence lingers
a rippling whisper.
So much empty air
and ancient slanting sunlight
through rainbowed glass,
and dust,
and memories of prayer.

We stay a moment
hushed by all this grandeur
built for one man's simple agony
and death;
try to feel stirred, or awed, or bowed
amidst the mouldy Bible smell –
but turn towards the light instead;
the endless hillsides' endless breath.

Stephen Bowkett
(Wales)

Morning and Evening

Sunbeams through twinkling pinewoods cast
Their shadows on my window screen.
A night of clouds and rain is past
And, newly blue and freshly green,
The Dawn rebuilds my world at last.
Pear-tree and plum-tree shed their burden sweet,
And children's happy voices rouse the street.

Wen T'ung
(China)

The Pond

There was this pond in the village
and little boys, he heard till he was sick,
were not allowed too near.
Unfathomable pool, they said,
that swallowed men and animals just so;
and in its depths, old people said,
swam galliwasps and nameless horrors;
bright boys kept away.

Though drawn so hard by prohibitions,
the small boy, fixed in fear, kept off;
till one wet summer, grass growing lush,
paths muddy, slippery, he found himself
there, at the fabled edge.

The brooding pond was dark.
Sudden, escaping cloud, the sun
came bright; and, shimmering in guilt,
he saw his own face peering from the pool.

Mervyn Morris
(Jamaica)

Lammas, Scotland's Harvest Time

We give thanks for a summer
that has been long and warm.
The sun has ripened the oats,
the stalks stand tall as hare on his back legs.

And now today,
on a dry, windless mid-August morning,
the reaping begins.

We dress as if for church on Sunday.
Clean shirts and blouses,
best clothes and polished shoes,
then walk in procession to the fields.

Our father turns to face the high white sun,
he takes off his cap
and places it gently on the ground.

With his sharp sickle he slices
a handful of corn and he whirls it
three times sunwise around his head.
Everyone cheers this first cut of harvest,
as the dust puffs drift in the sunlight.

All day long our family, our kin,
our friends and our neighbours praise
the God of the Harvest with songs and pipe tunes
as the women slice the corn
and the men bind the sheaves.

And in the evening, a myth-moon
rises mightily over the mountain.

John Rice
(Scotland)

The Modern Man

I came
And laughed at my father –
He
with his sideburns
Smelling of bear's grease
His coat
like that of the gentleman
whose image
is on tobacco tins
His watch-chain
and boots!
God!
how ridiculous he looked?

I
with my moustache
like Gable's
My sports coat
like Taylor's
My blue suede shoes

Today
My son came
And laughed at me.

Basil McFarlane
(Jamaica)

Boy on a Swing

Slowly he moves
to and fro, to and fro,
then faster and faster
he swishes up and down.

His blue shirt
billows in the breeze
like a tattered kite.

The world whirls by:
east becomes west,
north turns to south;
the four cardinal points
meet in his head.

    Mother!
Where did I come from?
When will I wear long trousers?
Why was my father jailed?

Oswald Mtshali
(South Africa)

Preparing to Travel

In my suitcase
I pack
neither clothes nor shoes

I take
the mountain and valley
so that
nothing will happen
behind my back
Not summer nor winter

Elisabeth Borchers
(Germany)

Glorious It Is

Glorious it is to see
The caribou flocking down from the forests
And beginning
Their wanderings to the north.
Timidly they watch
For the pitfalls of man.
Glorious it is to see
The great herds from the forests
Spreading out over plains of white.

Glorious it is to see
Early summer's short-haired caribou
Beginning to wander.
Glorious to see them trot
To and fro
Across the promontories.
Seeking for a crossing place.

Glorious it is
To see great musk oxen
Gathering in herds.
The little dogs they watch for
When they gather in herds.
Glorious to see.

Glorious it is
To see the long-haired winter caribou
Returning to the forests.
Fearfully they watch
For the little people,
While the herd follows the ebb-mark of the sea
With a storm of clattering hooves.
Glorious it is
When wandering time tiso come.

Traditional
(Inuit*)

*Inuit people live in areas around the Arctic
Circle (such as Greenland and Alaska)

There is No Word for Goodbye

Sokoya*, I said, looking through
    the net of wrinkles into
    wise black pools
    of her eyes.

What do you say in Athabaskan
    when you leave each other?
    What is the word
    for goodbye?

A shade of feeling rippled
    the wind-tanned skin.
    Ah, nothing, she said,
    watching the river flash.

She looked at me close.
 We just say, Tiaa. That means,
 See you.
 We never leave each other.
 When does your mouth
 say goodbye to your heart?
  She touched me light
  as a bluebell.
  You forget when you leave us
  You're so small then.
  We don't use that word.
  We always think you're coming back,
  But if you don't,
  we'll see you someplace else.
  You understand.
  There is no word for goodbye.

Mary TallMountain
(USA)

*Sokoya means aunt (mother's sister)

Mango, Little Mango

The mango stands for Africa
    in its taste
    in its smell
    in its colour
    in its shape

The mango has the shape of a heart –
    Africa too!
It has a reddy-brown shade
like the tanned plains
of my beloved earth.
Because of this I love you and your taste
    Mango!
Heart of fruit, sweet and mild.

You are the love of Africa
Because beating in your breast
    is Africa's heart,
    oh mango, little mango,
    love of Africa!

Anon.
(Sao Tomé and Principe)

Ya Jammal (O Camel Driver)

When the camel driver decided to leave he grieved my heart.
To him I said: have patience, O camel driver!
My patience is at an end, he said.

Where are you heading for? I said.
To the desert of the south, he said.
What are you carrying in your load? I said.
Chewing gum and perfume, he said.
What is ailing you? I said.
Longing for the beloved, he said.
Have you seen a physician? I said.
Ninety physicians, he said.
Take me with you, I said.
I can't my load is heavy, he said.
I can walk, I said.
My way is too long, he said.
I beseech you!
I can walk for a thousand years, I said.
Gentle dove! The life of a traveller is bitter, he said.

As the camel driver decided to leave, he grieved my heart.
And all that is left after him
are tears flowing down my cheeks.

Tawfig Zayyad
(Palestine)

The Little Trumpet

All that is left
of the magic of the fair
is this little trumpet
of blue and green tin,
blown by a girl
as she walks, barefoot, through the fields.
But within its forced note
are all the clowns, white ones and red ones,
the band all dressed in gaudy gold,
the merry-go-round, the calliope, the lights.
Just as in the dripping of the gutter
is all the tearfulness of the storm
the beauty of lightning and the rainbow;
and in the damp flickers of a firefly
whose light dissolves on a heather branch
is all the wondrousness of spring.

Corrado Govoni
(Italy)

Dew on a Spider Web

Two twigs acting as a loom
Hold a wonderful weaving.
Silver threads, simple but beautiful against the
bright blue sky.
Who would ever think this was woven by an ugly
   old spider?
How I would like to have a wonderful weaving
   like that.
My one would never fade away.

Michael Stone, age 10
(New Zealand)

The Song of Wandering Aengus

I went out to the hazel wood,
Because a fire was in my head,
And cut and peeled a hazel wand,
And hooked a berry to a thread;
And when white moths were on the wing,
And moth-like stars were flickering out,
I dropped the berry in a stream
And caught a little silver trout.

When I had laid it on the floor
I went to blow the fire a-flame,
But something rustled on the floor,
And someone called me by my name:
It had become a glimmering girl
With apple blossom in her hair
Who called me by my name and ran
And faded through the brightening air.

Though I am old with wandering
Through the hollow lands and hilly lands,
I will find out where she has gone,
And kiss her lips and take her hands;
And walk among long dappled grass,
And pluck till time and times are done
The silver apples of the moon,
The golden apples of the sun.

W. B. Yeats   (Ireland)

Day by Day I Float
My Paper Boats

Day by day I float my paper boats one by one down the
   running stream.
In big black letters I write my name on them and the
   name of the village where I live.
I hope that someone in some strange land will find them
   and know who I am.
I load my little boats with shiuli flowers from our
   garden, and hope that these blooms of the dawn will
   be carried safely to land in the night . . .

Rabindranath Tagore
(India)

INDEX OF FIRST LINES

INDEX OF POETS

ACKNOWLEDGEMENTS

The publishers wish to thank the following for permission to use copyright material:

Opal Palmer Adisa, 'After the Storm', included in *Hello New*, ed, John Agard, Orchard (2000), by permission of the author; **John Agard**, 'A Shell Awakening from Sleep', by permission of Caroline Sheldon Literary Agency on behalf of the author; **Moira Andrew**, 'The Naming Ceremony' from *Patchwork of Poems* by Moira Andrew, Folens (2000), and 'What Is Snow?' (2003), by permission of the author; **Leo Aylen**, 'Mother Without a Husband', first published in *Return to Zululand*, Sidgwick and Jackson, by permission of the author; **Matsuo Basho**, 'A baby crab...' and 'Winter downpour...' from *On Love and Barley: Haiku of Basho*, trans. Lucien Stryk, Penguin Classic (1985). Copyright © Lucien Stryk, 1985, by permission of Penguin Books; **James Berry**, 'A Nest Full of Stars'. Copyright © James Berry, by permission of The Peters Fraser and Dunlop Group Ltd on behalf of the author; **Clare Bevan**, 'Long Division Lesson', by permission of the author; **Ana Blandiana**, 'Hunt', trans. Seamus Heaney, by permission of Seamus Heaney; **Valerie Bloom**, 'Don' Ride No Coconut Bough Down Dere' and 'Heather', by permission of the author; **Elisabeth Borchers**, 'Preparing to Travel' from *Fish Magic: Selected Poems* by Elizabeth Borchers, trans. Anneliese Wagner (1989), by permission of Anvil Press Poetry and Anneliese Wagner; **Stephen Bowkett**, 'Coal Tip Mountain' and 'Inside the Church', by permission of the author; **Dave Calder**, 'Citizen of the World' by permission of the author; **Rosalia Castro**, 'The Bells' from *Spanish Poetry*, ed. and trans. by Eugenio Florit (1971), by permission of Dover Publications, Inc.; **Nirendranath Chakrabarti**, 'Amalkanti' from *The Oxford Anthology of Modern Indian Poetry*, ed. Vinay Dharwadker and A. K. Ramanujan, by permission of Oxford University Press India, New Delhi; **Debjani Chatterjee**, 'Mele Menagerie' and 'Square Peg' from *Animal Antics* by Debjani Chatterjee, Pennine Press (2000), by permission of the author; **Po Chu-I**, 'In Yung-Yang' from *A Feast of Lanterns*, by permission of John Murray (Publishers) Ltd; **Jane Clarke**, 'Finding a Friend', first published in *I Wanna be Your Mate*, ed. Tony Bradman, Bloomsbury Publishing Plc (1999), by permission of the author; **John Clarke**, 'My Feet are Killing Me', by permission of the author; **Alonso Damaso**, 'The Star Counters' from *Spanish Poetry*, ed. and trans. by Eugenio Florit (1971), by permission of Dover Publications, Inc; **Gina Douthwaite**, 'Christmas Across', first published in *New Reading 360*, Ginn